I Declare!

Speak Life & Prepare for Overflow

Dr. Leah McCray

ISBN: 9781520683782
ISBN-13:

Introduction

Do not allow yourself to be defined by your past. Decide to define yourself and your life by the word of God.

These prayers & declarations are a compilation from the end of each day in my *100 Words in 100 Days for a changed life and restored Purpose* devotional. Speak these prayers and declarations every morning, mid-day or evening. Get them in your heart and be in expectation of the anointing and power that you will begin to walk in.

Prayers & Declarations

I will believe the word that God has confirmed in my heart. I agree with God that my faith for it is the evidence of its manifestation. I will not allow what I see or don't see to shake my faith in God because my faith is based on His Word, not on what I see.

God loves me, and He is not angry with me. I have been cleansed, forgiven and made righteous by the blood of Jesus. No weapon formed against me can prosper. I cast all of my cares on my God because He cares for me.

Sickness is a curse, and I have <u>been</u> <u>redeemed</u> from the curse. Jesus bore my sickness on the cross. He took my pain, weaknesses, and punishment so that I would not have to bear them
By His stripes, I am healed. I walk in total healing and divine health NOW.

Poverty is a curse. I have been redeemed from the curse by the blood of Jesus. Jesus became poor so that I could be rich in all things, spiritual and material. I believe the Word of God over what I see before me.

I am prosperous because all things are in Christ and Christ is in me. I have been redeemed from the curse of poverty. He came to give me life and life more abundantly in every way. I believe His word on prosperity and I receive it by faith.

I will hope in the promise of your Word because you are faithful. My hope in your Word causes me to be in expectation and not worry. I thank you, God, that you do not put to shame anyone whose hope is in you.

God loves me and has promised never to forsake me. Jesus died for me on the cross because of His love for me. I am safe in His love.

I declare that through God's grace, I am empowered to do everything that He has purposed for my life.

Father, I am committed to obeying your instructions. If I have not obeyed any of the instructions that you have given me, please forgive me. I ask you to please give them to me again, and I will obey you. I thank you for giving me the power to carry out your word. I thank you, God, that as I carry out your instructions, you will make my way prosperous.

Father, I thank you that I have been made free by the blood of Jesus. I thank you that my sin debt is canceled and that I am justified and made righteous in Christ, Jesus. I will remember that Christ has given me the victory over sin and shame when the enemy tries to condemn me.

I rest in the finished work of my Lord and Savior, and I am hidden in Him, even right now. I thank you that I walk in the fruit of peace, love, and joy. Shame has no place in my life for I have been made right by the blood of Jesus.

I have the mind of Christ. I have control over my thoughts; therefore I will think only those thoughts that line up with the Word of God. Negative thoughts are from the enemy, and I will cast them down immediately. I will think good thoughts about myself, my life and others.

I thank you, Father, that I am free from guilt and shame. Jesus became sin for me, and He took all of my punishment on the cross.

Condemnation is from the enemy, and I do not allow it in my life. I thank you, Lord, for the conviction that leads me back to you if I disobey your word. Help me to be quick to repent so that guilt and condemnation will have no entrance into my life.

Failure is a thing of the past. God says that I am above only and not below; the head and not the tail. I am more than a conqueror in Christ, Jesus. I am a success because the Lord of Glory is prospering my way.

Father, I thank you for being the light that illuminates my path and please reveal to me any necessary turns or adjustments that I need to make. Thank you for giving me the opportunity to repent when I have missed it with you.

I thank you that I do not journey in this life alone, that you are with me to show me the way that I should go. I trust you, Lord, to guide me and direct my steps as I purpose to know your will in my life.

Father, help me to live a life that honors you. I will treat all people with honor because I will look at them through your eyes and not my own. I will honor others because you have commanded me to do so and my desire is to be obedient to your word and your will. I thank you that in honoring others, I please you.

Father, I thank you that you complete me. I thank you, Lord, that although it is your desire to give me many good things; when I have you, I have everything. Help me to know that in you, I lack no good thing and that I can be full every day and never empty.

You have called me to be salt and light. Lord, help me to exhibit these properties every day of my life. Thank you, Lord, that it is your power in me that gives me the ability and will to live for you. Father, I submit my will to you, and I ask that you continue to release your glory in my life so that I may be a reflection of you.

I am free and have liberty in Christ, Jesus. The enemy has been defeated by the work that Jesus accomplished on the cross. Christ is in the Father, and I am in Christ, nothing is impossible for me if I believe. The enemy does not limit me, but I will accomplish all the purposes that God has for my life.

Jesus has given me His peace. I speak peace over my life and in every situation. This peace that I have is from God, and nothing can take it away from me.

Father, I thank you for every season of my life for I know that you have purpose in them and will work all things for my good. I ask that you give me discernment to know and understand what I should be gleaning from this time in my life. I thank you that I have the mind of Christ and that I do not walk in confusion.

Thank you, Father, for the authority that you have given me in the earth. I command anything in my life that was not planted by you to be uprooted in the Name of Jesus. I thank you that I have the Spirit of Life reigning in my body and I call any and all things that are not of you to exit my life right now. I call forth healing, prosperity, peace, and joy as I walk in a deeper revelation of you each day.

I will keep my eyes on Jesus at all times, no matter what may be happening in my life. God has said that He will work everything that happens in my life for my good and His glory. I believe the Word of God and I judge Him faithful in all things. Father, help me to keep my eyes on you and not be distracted by the enemy.

Father, I declare that I do not allow frustration to dominate my emotions. I trust you, and I trust your timing for I know that you love me and that you are for me. I believe your word and I place my faith in your promises. I thank you that your word shall never return void.

I thank you, Father, that I walk in the joy of you today and every day. Help me always to remember that I am blessed no matter what it looks like and that I am blessed to be a blessing.

Father, help me to hear you clearly. I bind the voices of the world and the enemy that would try to speak lies into my life.

I resist any voices that are not of God, and I hear and hearken only to His voice. I resist the enemy at every turn. The enemy cannot gain a stronghold in my life because I tear down any alters that the enemy has erected by the word of God. I am strong in the Lord, and I am more than a conqueror in Christ, Jesus.

Father, help me to resist tolerance. Help me to esteem your word above all else. I believe that your word is true and anything that is contrary to your word is a lie. I will stand on your word, and I will be an example of your love and faithfulness to all those around me. Thank you for giving me the strength to resist the pull of the enemy, this world and my flesh.

Thank you, Father, for your precious Holy Spirit that leads me. Help me to hear your voice clearly and to hearken to your Word. Thank you for directing my steps today and every day.

Thank you, Father, for forgiving my sins. Thank you that I do not have to walk under condemnation for Jesus has paid the price for my sin. I refuse to have a guilty conscience, but I will repent quickly when convicted by your precious Holy Spirit. Thank you for redeeming me from the curse of the law which included guilt and shame. I walk in the newness of life by the blood and body of Jesus.

I will contend for the faith every day. I believe every word that God has spoken over my life. I give no weight to the circumstances or situations in my life. I give the greatest weight to what God says. God has given me the victory, in Christ, Jesus.

I see the attacks of the enemy clearly in my life because God gives me discernment. I resist the enemy's lies with the word of God. No weapon shall prosper against me because I stand on the word of God.

Thank you, Lord, that you are perfecting everything that concerns me. I cast all my cares upon you because I know that you care for me. Bless me to rest in your perfecting ways and to trust completely in you.

Father, I thank you that you are Jehovah Jireh, my provider. I thank you that you have promised to supply all of my needs and that you know what they are even before I bring them to you. I rest in your provision, Lord, and I thank you for your Word.

Father, help me to discipline myself according to your word. Help me to know that I have authority over my flesh and that I can accomplish all that you have set out for me to do. I declare that I hear your voice clearly and that I am quick to obey. I declare that I will bear much fruit in the earth and that I will walk by faith. Lord, help me to walk according to my faith today!

Father, help me to put action to my belief in your word. I declare that I will not be a just hearer of your word, but a doer also. Thank you that I will act upon the word of God that I hear and I will reap the blessing.

Father, help me never to step ahead of you. Help me to expectantly wait on your promise. Your timing is perfect, and I will not substitute my timetable for yours. I declare, by faith, that I seek your instructions and I will wait for your directions. I declare that I will rest in your word and look ahead with great joy and expectancy to the fulfilling of your word in my life.

Thank you, Father, that I am a new creation. The old things have passed away, and I have been made new. I walk in newness of life, and I am made free from the sin and guilt of the past. I declare that I am no longer held captive by the enemy but that I am a servant of God, joint-heir with my Lord and Savior, Jesus.

Father, help me to assess myself in you properly. Show me any areas of my life where I may be missing it and give me the plan to correct it. I thank you that you love me and that you desire me to live in fellowship with you. I declare that anything crooked in my life will be made straight by the power of God which lives in me by Christ Jesus.

Father, help me to enter into your rest. I declare that I will cast every care at your feet and that I will not try to fight my own battles. I thank you that I have already achieved victory in this life by your redemptive work on the cross. I agree with you that it is finished and I rest in the victory that you have obtained for me.

Father, help me to walk in your wisdom and not the wisdom of man. I declare that I have the mind of Christ and that I will not succumb to the folly of men. Father, I ask for your wisdom in every situation, and I receive it by faith.

I declare that I do not stagger at the word of my God, but that I stand firmly upon it. I speak the life of His word into my life, and I reap the blessing of it. I do not walk in fear, but in power, love and soundness of mind, in Christ, Jesus.

I am strong in Jesus. The power of God in me is greater than anything in this world or anything that is coming against me. God is for me, and He has given me the victory.

Thank you, Jesus, for taking my place on the cross. I have been redeemed from the curse because Jesus became a curse for me. I have been made free from the law of sin and death by the blood and body of Christ.

Father, help me to be a better friend to you today by obeying your word and hearkening to your voice. Help me to be a friend to others by putting their needs above my own and practicing the selflessness that Jesus exhibited in His life. I declare that I will be the heart and hands of Jesus here on earth.

I declare that I am a living witness of the love and grace of Jesus on this earth. I show the love of God in everything that I say and do. I am a reflection of my Lord and Savior, and I can do this by the strength and grace of God

Father, teach me how to worship you in spirit and truth. Give me a heart of worship and a desire to place you first, far above all things. Help me to know that in you; I can find all that I need and that my dependence upon you *is* worship.

Father, I thank you that you have commanded your blessing upon my life. I declare to speak only your words over my life and to resist the lies of the enemy. I will speak life to myself and to

all those around me; the life that is in your word.

Father, help me to identify and to cast off any relationship that is not of you. Help me to be light in the midst of darkness and to lift you up so that all men may be drawn to you. I declare that I will not walk with darkness, but that I will be a bearer of the Word of God which is light and life.

I declare that I have been justified, set apart and made holy by the blood of the Lamb. I am the righteousness of Christ. I walk in the spiritual blessing of Abraham, even right now. I have been made whole and complete by the blood of Jesus.

Father, I thank you for saving me from your wrath. Thank you for the shed blood of Jesus that covers me and shields me from the attacks of the enemy. I ask that you would open the eyes of the blind and allow them to see the wonderful gift of your salvation. Give me opportunities to be a witness of your saving grace in the lives of others and to show them that the fear of you is the beginning of wisdom.

Father, create in me a clean heart; one that will not sin against you. Help me to repent quickly; to turn from my sin towards you. Reveal any strongholds of sin or wrong thinking in my life and give me the strategy to tear it down. Thank you that you are the Lord of my life and that I have victory in you.

Father, let my desires be your desires. Bless me to run after them with faith and patience. I declare that I will delight myself in you, putting you first in everything.

I thank you, Father, that I am secure in Jesus. I declare and agree with your word that no weapon formed against me shall prosper. I declare that I have received the gift of salvation by faith and that as Jesus is, so am I in this world.

Jesus has secured my salvation and has defeated death and the plans of the enemy. Nothing can separate me from the love of God. He has promised never to leave me nor forsake me.

Father, help me to receive all of your promises in my life. Thank you for the gift of salvation, and all that comes with that gift.

I declare miracles, signs and wonders to follow the word of my God. I declare that I will see these things in my life and the life of others.

Father, help me to identify any areas of pride in my life and to cast it down by your word. I declare that pride has no place in my life and that I walk in the humility of God. I boast in the works and word of God only, and not in myself.

Father, help me to identify the source of all my thoughts and actions. I declare to cast down and resist anything that is not of you in my life. I will resist evil with your word, and I will speak life into every situation. I decide to walk in the light of your word and not in the darkness and ignorance.

Father, help me to make a difference in this world. Thank you that I do not have to conform to this world but that I am transformed by the power of your word. I declare that I am a change agent by the power of the Holy Spirit.

Father, I pray for the lost everywhere. Let the scales be removed from their eyes and give them a moment of clarity.

I ask that they would begin to see their sin and their need for a savior. Bless me with an opportunity to tell someone of your goodness today.

I declare that we are not ignorant of the tactics of the enemy! In Jesus Name! I declare that I see the tactics of the enemy and I resist them in the Name of Jesus. I rest in the provision of God's word and take authority over the tactics of the enemy. I am victorious in life by the blood of Jesus.

Father, help me to identify wrong associations and to free myself of them. Help me to be salt and light in this world and to obey your word. I declare that I will not value the accolades of men but will only seek to be pleasing in your sight.

Father, allow me to see with my spiritual eyes and not be tricked by the prince of this world. I declare that I believe what I see in the word of God and what I see in the spirit over what I see in the natural realm. Thank you, Father, for perfecting my vision.

I declare that I will wait on the Lord. I will not manipulate people and circumstances to further my own desires, but I will wait on the perfect timing of God. I trust in His word, and I will not fear.

Father, help me to recognize your headship in every area of my life. I declare to exalt the name of Jesus above everything in my life. I will put your word above all else.

Father, help me to stand on your word. I declare that I will speak your words only over my life and that I will speak them in faith. I declare to agree with your word and to stand against the arguments and tactics of the enemy.

Father thank you for restoring those barren, dead places in my life!

Father, I thank you that I will not be moved by what I see but only by your Holy Spirit and your Word. I place my trust and faith in you only, and I declare that your word shall not return void.

I declare that I will move when you say move and that I will achieve all that you have purposed for my life. I declare that I choose life over death. Jesus is the rock of my life, and I build the foundation of my life upon His sacrifice on the cross.

Father, I thank you for your vision, and I purpose to run after it with all my heart. I declare that I will purpose to do your will and that I will be a blessing to those that you have attached to my life. I declare that I walk with purpose and that I will redeem the time that you have given me.

I praise you because you are God. I will magnify you with the praise of my lips and the love shed abroad in my heart. I will boast of you all the day long. You are a good God, and I give you praise.

I thank you that I have been made free in you. I have am redeemed from the law, and I am no longer a slave to sin, by the blood of Jesus.

Father, help me to trust in your provision and your word. I declare that I will not fear lack and will give the tithe and offering as commanded by God and, as a result, I will walk under open heavens. Freely I have received, and freely I give.

I will magnify the Lord at all times; His praise shall continually be on my lips. I will not walk in fear, but I will magnify my God over everything that I see before me. My God is bigger than all and I rest in His provision and care.

I respect those who are in authority over me, even if I disagree with them. I trust God to reward my obedience to His word and have confidence in His faithfulness. For He has commanded us to love each other with genuine affection and to take delight in honoring one another.

I declare to set my heart on your word and your purposes in my life. I will seek first your kingdom and its righteousness; believing that as I do this, you will take care of everything that concerns me.

I declare that I will be led by the Spirit of God and not be tossed to and fro by a spirit of confusion. I am the redeemed of the Lord. I walk in the blessing of Abraham, and I have been redeemed from the curse.

Thank you, Father, that I am not defined by my past but by your word. I am a new creation in Christ, and I walk in newness of life. Thank you, Father, that you have made me free indeed!

I place my confidence and trust in the Lord, my God. I stand on His word in faith. I do not believe the report of the enemy; I only believe the word of God.

I declare that I will not be tricked by the shadows of the enemy. I will trust in the Lord with all my heart, and I am victorious in His word.

Father, help me to understand that I do not have to fight the battles in life on my own. Help me to know that you fight for me and secure the victory on my behalf. I declare to wait on your instructions and not to panic or make decisions in fear when trials enter my life. I trust in you, my God, and I rest in the victory that you provide.

Thank you for the blood of Jesus that has washed away my sins and secured my forgiveness forever. I declare that just as God has forgiven me, I will forgive anyone that has hurt me.

I walk in the favor of God. I have favor with God and man. I thank God for His grace and His favor.

Father, help me to judge myself so that you will not have to judge me. Help me to not judge others. I declare that I walk free from the judgment of others and that I walk in the freedom that God has provided for me.

Father, help me not to be careless with the gifts that you have given me. I purpose to use my gifts to further your Kingdom and to be a blessing to others. Thank you, Father, for making all things work together for my good.

I declare to always to give you praise and to trust in your unfailing love. Thank you for the victorious and abundant life that you have purposed for me.

Father, please forgive me for ever causing another to feel shame. I am an ambassador of your grace, and I purpose to show your love to everyone that I meet. I thank you for the grace to do this, in Christ Jesus.

Father, help me to deny myself daily and to live out your purposes in my life.

I purpose not to have a form of godliness but to be empowered by your word. I purpose to give you all the glory for every good thing that happens in my life for I know that all good and perfect gifts are from you.

I am made in God's image and likeness. I have been purchased by the precious blood of Jesus. God loves me, and I am the apple of His eye.

I do not waver or doubt the word of God. I walk in faith, and I receive all of the promises of God by faith and patience.

Jesus defeated sin and death on the cross. Therefore it has no hold over me. I have eternal life by the blood of Christ that was shed on my behalf. By the power of God that resides in me by Christ Jesus, I no longer walk in fear of death or the enemy for I have put the enemy under my feet.

Father, I thank you that all of your promises are mine by faith. I believe that you are the same God yesterday, today and forever, therefore I expect to see miracles, signs and wonders now just like in times past. I thank you that your power to deliver has not lessened over time. You are God, and there is nothing too hard for you.

Enjoy these other books by

Dr. Leah McCray

100: 100 Words in 100 Days
Devotional

The Kingdom Wife

Not Today, Satan

Made in the USA
Monee, IL
09 July 2021

73258149R00025